Meet NASA Inventor Dava Newman and Her Team's

Second-Skin Space Suit

WORLD
BOOK

www.worldbook.com

World Book, Inc.
180 North LaSalle Street
Suite 900
Chicago, Illinois 60601
USA

For information about other World Book publications, visit our website at www.worldbook.com or call 1-800-WORLDBK (967-5325).

For information about sales to schools and libraries, call 1-800-975-3250 (United States), or 1-800-837-5365 (Canada).

Produced in collaboration with the National Aeronautics and Space Administration (NASA).

Library of Congress Cataloging-in-Publication Data for this volume has been applied for.

Out of This World
ISBN: 978-0-7166-6261-7 (set, hc.)

Second-Skin Space Suit
ISBN: 978-0-7166-6264-8 (hc.)

Also available as:
ISBN: 978-0-7166-6272-3 (e-book)

Printed in USA by Corporate Graphics
1st printing May 2021

Staff

Editorial

Director
Tom Evans

Manager, New Content
Jeff De La Rosa

Writer
William D. Adams

Proofreader/Indexer
Nathalie Strassheim

Graphics and Design

Senior Visual Communications Designer
Melanie Bender

Media Researcher
Rosalia Bledsoe

Acknowledgments

Cover	© Victor Habbick Visions/Getty Images	35	© Matuska/Shutterstock; MIT
4-5	© Delpixel/Shutterstock	36-37	MIT
6-7	© Mark Garlick, Science Photo Library	38-39	© Twentieth Century Fox; © Fox 2000 Pictures
8-9	© Dotted Yeti/ Shutterstock	40-41	NASA
10-11	© Detlev van Ravenswaay, Science Source	42-43	© Dotted Yeti/Shutterstock
12-13	NASA/JPL-Caltech/MSSS	44	Julia Cort/WGBH; Dava Newman
15	Dava Newman		
16-17	© Artsiom Petrushenka, Shutterstock		
18-21	NASA		
23-25	© Shutterstock		
26-27	© Twentieth Century Fox; NASA		
29	Bill Ingalls, NASA		
31	Aerospace Medical Research Laboratories		
32-33	Dava Newman		

Contents

Glossary There is a glossary of terms on page 45. Terms defined in the glossary are in boldface type that **looks like this** on their first appearance on any spread (two facing pages).

Pronunciations (how to say words) are given in parentheses the first time some difficult words appear in the book. They look like this: pronunciation (pruh NUHN see AY shuhn).

Introduction

Clothing is not just about fashion. The clothes
we wear help to protect our bodies and keep us
comfortable. In cold places, people wear thick
coats, hats, and gloves to stay warm. People in
warm environments wear lighter clothing, often
in bright colors to reflect the sun's heat.

Temperature is not the only factor people keep
in mind when getting dressed, either. In hot and
dry deserts, for example, people often cover up
head to toe to protect their skin from sunburn.

Workers in extreme environments often require
additional protective gear. Firefighters, for

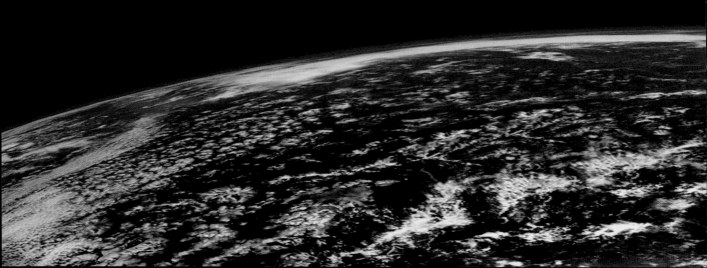

example, wear thick coats, boots, helmets, and masks to protect themselves from flames, smoke, and other hazards.

Perhaps nobody works in more extreme environments than do astronauts. Astronauts can be exposed to intense heat and cold, dangerous **radiation,** and even the **vacuum** of space. An astronaut's clothing must provide protection from these hazards and more. But it also must supply life-giving oxygen and other necessities. Astronauts thus rely on clothing for more than comfort and protection—their clothes literally keep them alive.

A modern astronaut suit is a wonder of technology, providing for its wearer's every need. But all that functionality comes at a price. Numerous hoses, **sensors,** and wires must be crammed in with layers of different fabric, each serving a special purpose. And, everything must be airtight so the suit can be filled with air. The result can be bulky, uncomfortable, and downright clumsy.

The inventor Dava Newman is working to change that. Newman is developing the next generation of space suit—one that will use high-tech materials and other technologies to trim down the bulk of previous models. The result could be lighter, leaner, and more maneuverable than anything astronauts have worn before, enabling them to explore new frontiers—such as the surface of Mars—in safety, comfort, and maybe even a little style.

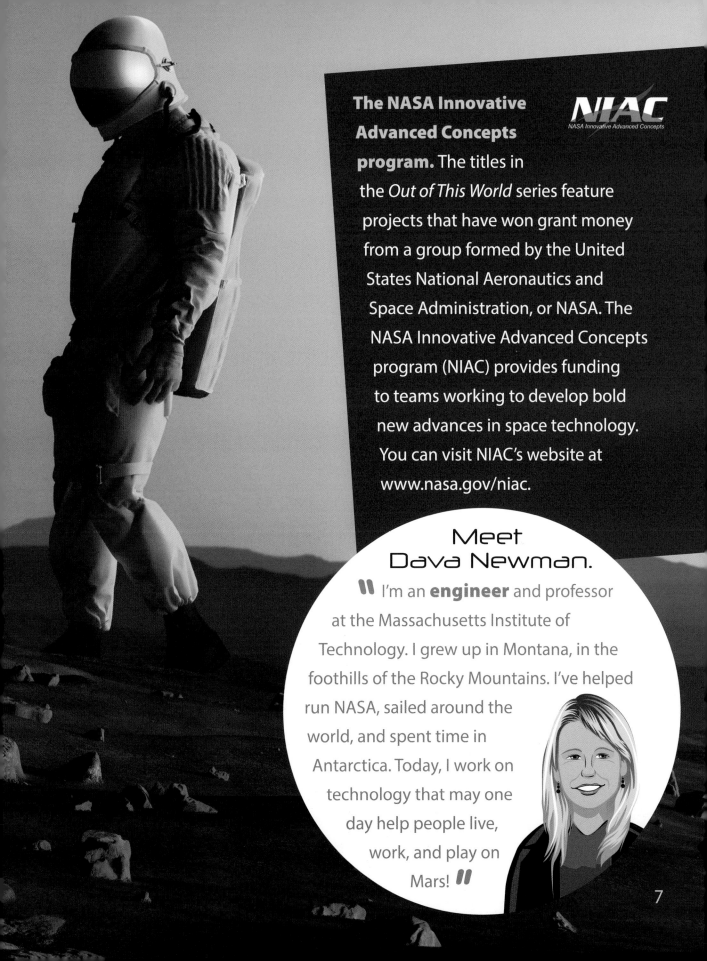

The NASA Innovative Advanced Concepts program. The titles in the *Out of This World* series feature projects that have won grant money from a group formed by the United States National Aeronautics and Space Administration, or NASA. The NASA Innovative Advanced Concepts program (NIAC) provides funding to teams working to develop bold new advances in space technology. You can visit NIAC's website at www.nasa.gov/niac.

Meet Dava Newman.

❚❚ I'm an **engineer** and professor at the Massachusetts Institute of Technology. I grew up in Montana, in the foothills of the Rocky Mountains. I've helped run NASA, sailed around the world, and spent time in Antarctica. Today, I work on technology that may one day help people live, work, and play on Mars! ❚❚

Destination: Mars

Most experts see the planet Mars as the next big destination for human space exploration.

II Why Mars? That's where we go to search for evidence of life. **II** —Dava

The surface of Mars may appear a cold, barren, and nearly airless desert. But billions of years ago, Mars was a different place than it is today. It was much warmer and had a thicker **atmosphere.** Oceans covered much of its surface. It is possible that simple forms of life arose there. Such life may have died out as the planet cooled and dried, or it could have retreated underground.

Since the late 1990's, a number of robotic rovers have explored the Martian surface. But rovers have their limits. Even the smallest of their movements must be carefully planned. And, rovers piloted from Earth are slow to react to changing conditions. A human astronaut on Mars could perform experiments and travel distances in a few days that would take a rover many years.

" We know the building blocks of life are on Mars, including seasonal water at the Martian surface. That's why it's so exciting! All of the evidence is mounting. " —Dava

Mars challenges

For human visitors, Mars presents many of the same challenges as Earth's moon. Among the most important is a relative lack of **atmosphere.** The atmosphere of Mars is about one percent as dense (thick) as that of Earth. As a result, astronauts will need two things from their suits: air supply and pressurization.

Air supply. With little atmosphere, astronauts will need air to breathe. Space suits provide oxygen to astronauts from tanks. But people also breathe out **carbon dioxide,** which is toxic in high doses. Therefore, space suits usually include special filters to remove carbon dioxide from the air the astronaut is breathing.

Pressurization. Breathing is not all our atmosphere is good for. The overlying weight of Earth's atmosphere provides a pressure on everything on the planet's surface, including our bodies. Our bodies are used to this pressure, and they need it to function normally. Without this pressure, bubbles of gas would form in an astronaut's blood and body tissues, expanding the body and causing severe pain, injury, and even death.

A mission to the Martian surface presents some additional challenges.

Cold. The surface of Mars is extremely chilly, about -80 °F (-60 °C) on average. An astronaut's suit will likely require some kind of heating system. Space suits sometimes incorporate battery powered heaters. These devices heat water, which is pumped through hoses sewn into the suit, distributing warmth to all parts of the astronaut's body.

Length of mission. Many modern space suits are designed to be worn for only a few hours. But Mars and Earth **orbit** the sun in such a way that there are limited opportunities to easily travel from one to the other. As a result, a human visit to the Martian surface would likely last for at least three months. Astronauts would probably spend dozens of hours walking on the surface over the course of many days. They would thus need space suits that are comfortable, durable, and easy to repair.

Gravity could prove both a blessing and a challenge. The force due to gravity at the Martian surface is about 38 percent that on Earth, making an astronaut feel much lighter. This fact could help an astronaut to maneuver in a somewhat heavier space suit. But astronauts will have to adjust their movements to account for the low gravity conditions.

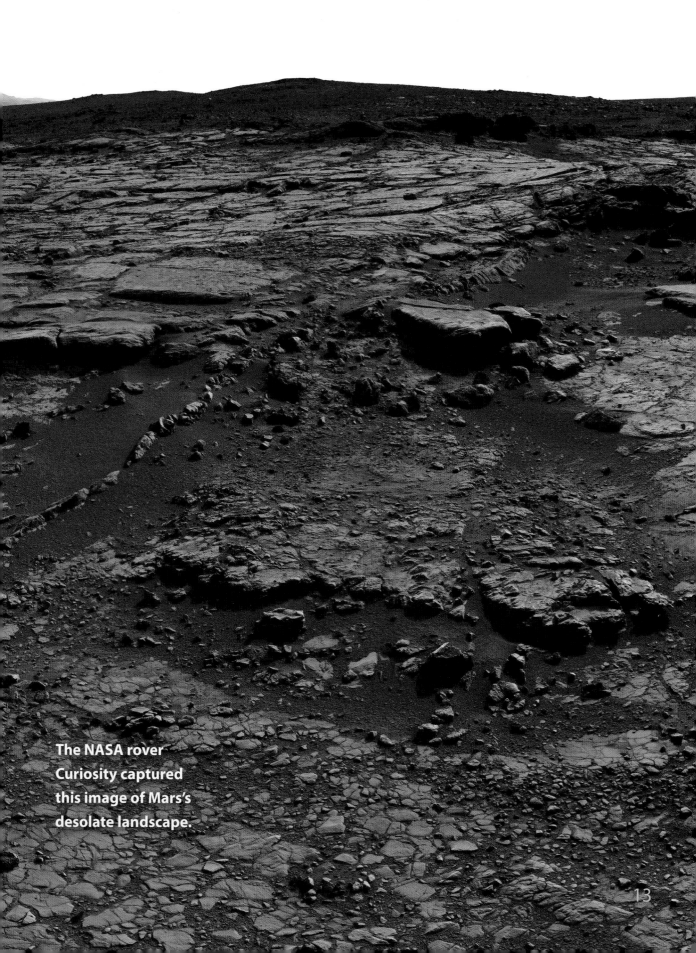

The NASA rover
Curiosity captured
this image of Mars's
desolate landscape.

Inventor feature:
Growing up

Newman comes from a family of teachers. She grew up in Helena, Montana, where she loved exploring the Rocky Mountains. Like many people her age, she was inspired by the Apollo missions, which landed astronauts on the moon in the 1960's and 1970's. Newman wasn't a big science fiction fan, but she loved the work of the French writer Jules Verne (1828-1905).

❚❚ How did he get everything right? ❚❚
—Dava

Verne's stories forecast the invention of airplanes, television, guided missiles, and space satellites. They were written in the 1800's, decades before such things existed!

Newman excelled at sports when she was growing up. She was a top-division ski racer in high school and played basketball at the University of Notre Dame in Indiana.

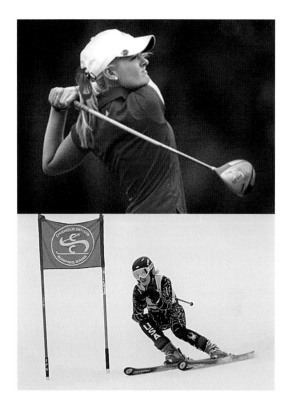

❚❚ I never thought my athletic career would dovetail with my academic training. ❚❚ —Dava

At first, she focused her studies around a career as a lawyer. But her older brother—himself a lawyer—knew she was destined for other things. He encouraged her to focus on science and **engineering.** After earning her bachelor's degree in **aerospace** engineering from Notre Dame, she completed two master's degrees and a Ph.D. degree in aerospace biomedical engineering at the Massachusetts Institute of Technology (MIT).

The EMU: The world's smallest spacecraft

The need to supply all that support and protection—to provide pressurization, heat, and everything else an astronaut needs—can result in an extremely bulky outfit. Just how bulky? Consider a state-of-the-art modern space suit: NASA's Extravehicular Mobility Unit (EMU). The EMU is the suit astronauts use to perform spacewalks outside the International Space Station (ISS), in **orbit** around Earth. Newman calls the EMU the world's smallest spacecraft.

EMU's have been used in dozens of missions. They enabled astronauts to repair the Hubble Space Telescope and construct the ISS. Astronauts use EMU's several times each year on spacewalks to maintain, repair, and upgrade the ISS.

Why not wear the EMU on Mars? In orbit, outside the ISS, the suit is effectively weightless. But it weighs a crushing 319 pounds (145 kilograms) on Earth. Even in the reduced **gravity** of Mars, it would be far too heavy for an astronaut to wear for long. In addition, astronauts on a spacewalk use their arms for crawling along a spacecraft. The EMU's "pants" are not even designed for walking.

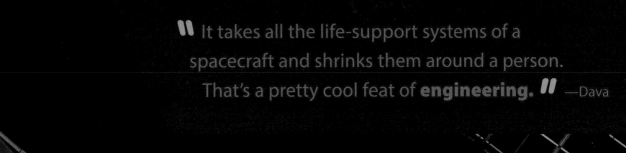

" It takes all the life-support systems of a spacecraft and shrinks them around a person. That's a pretty cool feat of **engineering.** " —Dava

The Apollo lunar suits were bulky
and cumbersome. Here, the
American geologist and astronaut
Harrison Schmitt loses his balance
during the Apollo 17 expedition.

Air pressure problems

The Extravehicular Mobility Unit (EMU) incorporates all kinds of special equipment, contributing to the suit's bulk. But perhaps the biggest contributor to its clumsiness is pressurization.

You may have seen video footage of Apollo astronauts gracefully bounding across the surface of the moon, planting the American flag, or working with equipment for experiments. In fact, there is far more footage of astronauts tripping, falling over, dropping things, and struggling to pick up the things they dropped.

Their suits were designed to provide one-third of Earth's air pressure at sea level—about what you'd feel at the top of Mount Everest, the world's tallest mountain. That is just enough for specially trained astronauts to work without getting sick or injured. But in the **vacuum** of space, even this lower pressure causes the space suit to swell up like a balloon. This swelling makes it difficult for the suit to move and bend.

An uncomfortable uniform

The Extravehicular Mobility Unit (EMU) is not just clumsy. It is downright uncomfortable. Many astronauts return from spacewalks with minor injuries. The painful badges of a few hours in the EMU can include bruises, scrapes, blisters, muscle strains, tendon sprains, and even detached fingernails.

Think of the EMU as a giant balloon with the astronaut floating inside. A spacewalking astronaut must push and pull against the suit to perform the slightest activity. The struggle can lead to injuries to the shoulders, neck, and sides.

Where do the fingernails come in? The fingers of a space suit are some of the hardest pieces to maneuver. The astronaut is constantly digging into them with the fingertips for leverage. If the astronaut's nails are not properly trimmed or the gloves are not sized correctly, the stress of moving the gloves around can cause the nail to separate from the finger. Ouch!

If astronauts are going to live and work on Mars for months or years, they will need comfortable, flexible space suits. It is not clear that a conventional, air-filled space suit will be up to the task.

Even a simple wave can be a difficult maneuver in the EMU.

Hard suits

If an inflated fabric suit makes it hard for an astronaut to move, why not make a suit out of rigid materials? That was the first approach Newman studied. Hard suits have pieces of metal or other materials connected by hinges and rotating seals. They solve the pressurization problem of soft suits, but they are just as hard or harder to move.

In 2002, chasing a lifelong dream, Newman set sail on a voyage around the world. She and her partner, Guillermo Trotti, sailed aboard a 47-foot (14.4-meter) boat named *Galatea* from January 2002 to June 2003. The voyage was part of the *Galatea* Odyssey Mission, an educational outreach program to children in the United States and around the world.

Such a journey is not without its perils. The pair lost their automatic steering in the middle of the Pacific Ocean.

❚❚ That was our Apollo 13 moment. ❚❚ —Dava

Apollo 13 was a famous 1970 space mission in which U.S. astronauts bound for the moon overcame a serious equipment malfunction to get back to Earth safely. Far from Earth, the astronauts survived in part through the creative use of materials they had on board.

Newman and Trotti were likewise many hundreds of miles or kilometers from rescue and had to repair *Galatea* with whatever they had on hand. For two days, they had to steer the ship by hauling on a heavy tiller—day and night—while they assessed the problem.

A tiny crack in a copper pipe had caused all the steering fluid to leak out. Luckily, they discovered that the olive oil Newman had bought during their journey had the same *viscosity* (fluid thickness or stickiness) as the steering fluid! They sealed the crack as best they could and filled the steering system with olive oil.

Dava Newman and her partner Guillermo Trotti aboard *Galatea*

Big idea:
Mechanical counterpressure

The human body requires pressure to function properly. But the pressure does not have to come from air.

❝ The only other feasible way is to apply pressure directly to the skin. ❞ —Dava

Have you ever sprained your ankle? You may have used a compression wrapping to make it feel better. A compression wrapping is an elastic bandage or sleeve wrapped around a limb or joint. The wrapping squeezes the body, providing extra support and pressure to reduce pain and *inflammation* (swelling).

What if you wrapped an astronaut's whole body in compression bandages? The compression from the bandages might replace the pressure provided by filling a space suit with air. This concept of applying pressure directly to the skin is called **mechanical counterpressure** (MCP).

Big idea:
Mechanical
counterpressure cont.

Imagine a skin-tight **mechanical counterpressure** (MCP)
space suit. It is easy to imagine that such a suit could be more
maneuverable than a bulky, air-filled suit. But an MCP suit might
also be more durable.

Think of how quickly a tire on a bicycle or automobile deflates
when punctured. Likewise, any damage to a conventional space
suit—from helmet to boot—will quickly cause its air to escape
into space. The astronaut inside might have to make a mad
dash for shelter before losing consciousness.

If an MCP suit is punctured or scraped, the astronaut might
suffer minor damage to the skin exposed—if it remains exposed
for too long—but that is all. The astronaut could easily apply a
special patch to the suit, probably while still out exploring.

The American scientist Paul Webb developed an experimental
MCP space suit as early as the 1960's and 1970's. However, the
design was limited by the materials available at the time, and

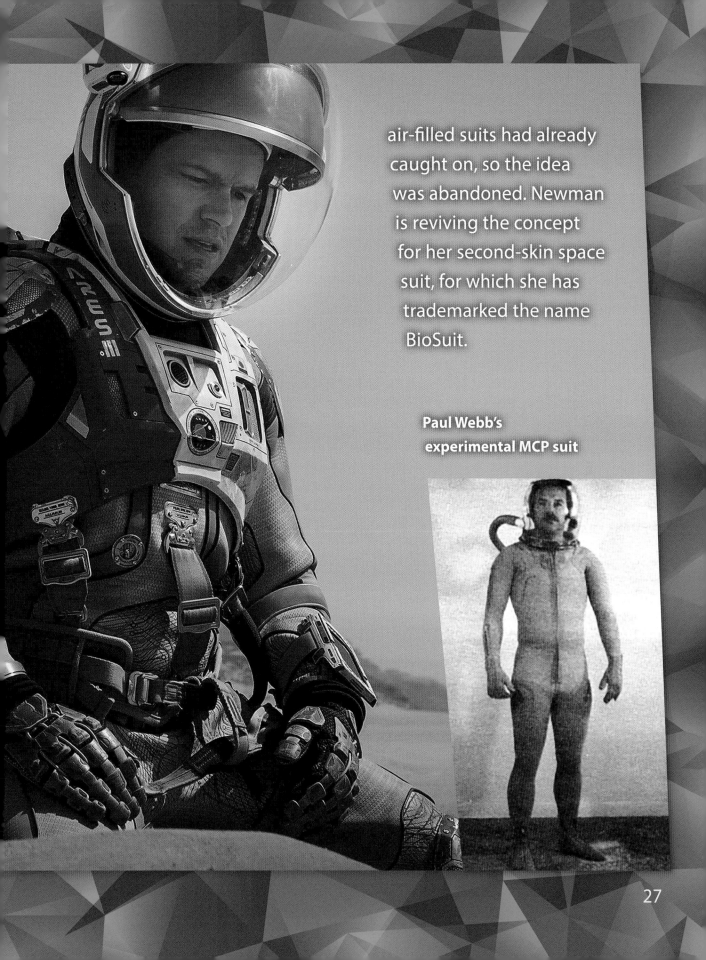

air-filled suits had already caught on, so the idea was abandoned. Newman is reviving the concept for her second-skin space suit, for which she has trademarked the name BioSuit.

Paul Webb's experimental MCP suit

Inventor feature:
Deputy Administrator of NASA

From April 2015 to January 2017, Newman served as Deputy Administrator of the United States National Aeronautics and Space Administration (NASA). This made her second in charge of the country's nonmilitary space program, working with administrator Charles Bolden.

During her time as deputy administrator, Newman prided herself on forming and growing partnerships. NASA partners with other government agencies, private companies, and more than 120 other countries to develop, build, and launch space missions.

Newman's duties as deputy administrator kept her very busy. And, her space suit designs could not be considered for development during her tenure to avoid even the appearance of favoritism. As a result, she did not work much on her BioSuit during this time.

While at NASA, Newman introduced the Lean Forward; Fail Smart award. This award honored NASA projects that, while not achieving the intended goal, helped researchers learn something important.

❚❚ We have to be okay with failure. That's where a lot of our great breakthroughs come from. As an **engineer,** I know I'm going to design something wrong the first eight times. Hopefully, on attempt nine or ten, I'll have something innovative to work with. ❚❚ —Dava

Dava Newman walks to a meeting with NASA Administrator Charles Bolden on her first day as deputy administrator.

Lines of nonextension

It takes much more than a bunch of elastic bandages to make a working space suit. On its own, such a suit would be too snug for an astronaut to move easily. But some ingenious **engineering** can make it feel as comfortable as a second skin.

The human body is extremely flexible. Almost every part of our skin bends and stretches when we move. But there are some bands of skin that, though they may twist and turn, never stretch. These bands are called **lines of nonextension.**

The American scientist Arthur Iberall developed the concept of lines of nonextension. He used this idea in developing pressure suits in the 1940's and 1950's. In such a suit, Iberall realized, strong, *inelastic* (nonstretching) cords, fibers, or wires can be strung along lines of nonextension without making it any harder for the wearer to move. Where lines of nonextension cross, these fibers can be bound together, creating a semirigid framework.

The result might look a little like the outfit of the superhero Spiderman, with a suit of flexible material supported by a web of inelastic cords.

Arthur Iberall's experimental pressure suits using lines of nonextension allowed for greater freedom of movement than traditional pressure suits.

a. Unpressurized

b. 2 psi

c. 3 psi

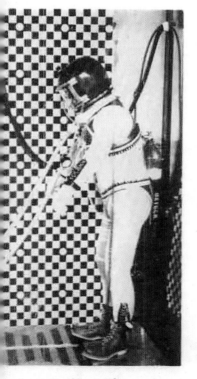

d. 3.75 psi

e. 3.75 psi

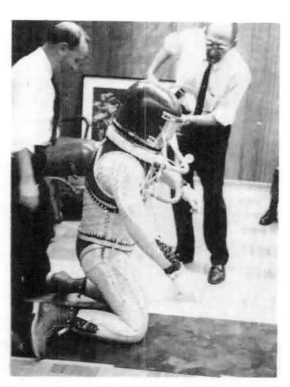

f. 3.75 psi

Figure 19

31

Newman recognized that Arthur Iberall's work on **lines of nonextension** could be combined with Paul Webb's work on **mechanical counterpressure** (MCP) to create a skin-tight space suit. The key ingredient lay in advanced materials not available during Iberall and Webb's time.

❝ Real advances in revolutionary technological capabilities led me to think about a second-skin space suit—shrink-wrapping the astronauts! It isn't science fiction—it turns out that it's technically feasible. ❞ —Dava

Newman and her team have found that everyone has lines of nonextension in similar patterns on their bodies. This should make it easy to create custom suits for a generation of new explorers.

Big idea:
Shape memory materials

One of the problems with **mechanical counterpressure** (MCP) suits is they must be extremely tight, making it difficult to put them on and take them off. To solve this problem, Newman is experimenting with **shape memory materials.**

Shape memory materials seem able to "remember" their shape, returning to it when heated, usually with electricity. Imagine a wire of shape memory metal that has been twisted into a spring. The wire might later be pulled straight again. But upon heating, it may return to its spring shape.

The ability of the material to "remember" its shape may seem mystical, but it is actually a result of atomic structure. The **atoms** or **molecules** of shape memory materials are arranged in a certain *configuration* (pattern), called *martensite*. Bending a piece of the material causes the

Down to Earth:

Ideas from space that could serve us on our planet.

Two identical shape memory springs in their stretched and contracted states (ring for scale)

atoms to change to another configuration, called *austenite*. When the material is heated to a certain temperature, the austenite areas return to martensite configuration, snapping the piece back to its original shape.

The technology behind the BioSuit may be able to help infants on Earth. Cerebral palsy is a group of disorders caused by damage to the brain during birth or in the first few years of life that result in a lack of muscle control. A newborn baby with cerebral palsy could wear BioSuit-like sleeves that guide the muscles to move more efficiently, helping the baby to develop muscle control.

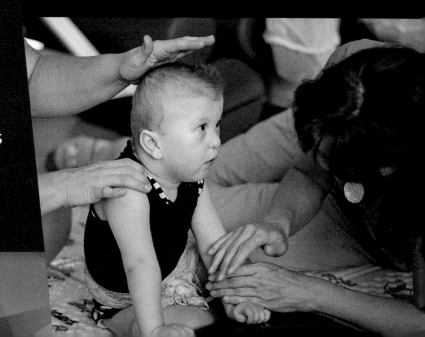

Using shape memory wire

Newman and her team have developed several ingenious uses for **shape memory materials.**

Newman's team placed thicker shape memory wires along **lines of nonextension** on the BioSuit. These wires are trained to a zigzag shape but are then bent back to straight to follow lines of nonextension. A special electric current is used as a "key" to get in or out of the suit. When the current is applied, the shape memory wires return to their zigzag shape, giving more slack to the elastic fibers connected to them and allowing an astronaut to slip into or out of the suit. When the current is stopped, the wires can be straightened, pulling the other fibers taut. It's almost like covering the suit in zippers to get that perfect tight fit!

Newman and her team have also bent and trained shape memory wires into springs. These springs can be used to reach the pressure needed to keep astronauts safe on the Martian surface.

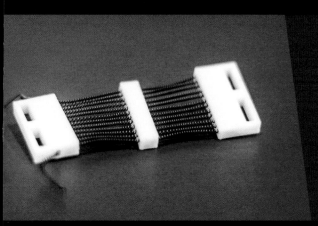

A close-up view of a 3-D-printed shape memory cartridge that packs 24 shape memory "zippers" into a 1-inch- (2.5-centimeter-) wide structure.

Such cartridges can be attached to fabric to create sections that cinch up when electric current is removed from the wires.

These shape memory cartridges are being developed for use in tourniquets for emergency medicine, to help stabilize wounds and reduce bleeding.

Inventor feature:
Reaching out

As part of her public outreach, Newman has gotten the opportunity to help with major motion pictures. She served as a science advisor on *The Martian* (2015), a science-fiction film about an astronaut stranded on Mars. The astronauts in the movie wear space suits inspired by Newman's BioSuit.

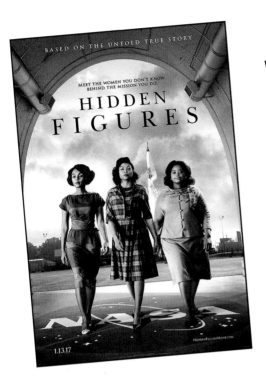

While serving as NASA Deputy Administrator, Newman also helped with *Hidden Figures* (2016). The movie told the true story of the African American women who performed critical calculations in the early stages of NASA's human space flight program during the 1960's.

Newman has written a textbook for college students called *Interactive Aerospace Engineering and Design* (2001). She had noticed that most books on aerospace **engineering** were written at graduate levels, but there wasn't a good introductory book for undergraduates.

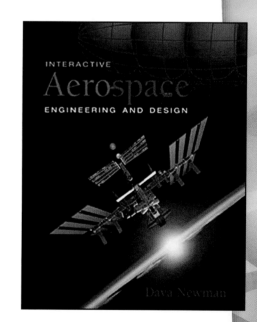

❚❚ When I was an undergraduate, I wish someone would have told me, 'Engineering is for you! Engineering is for everyone!' ❚❚ —Dava

Other functions of a space suit

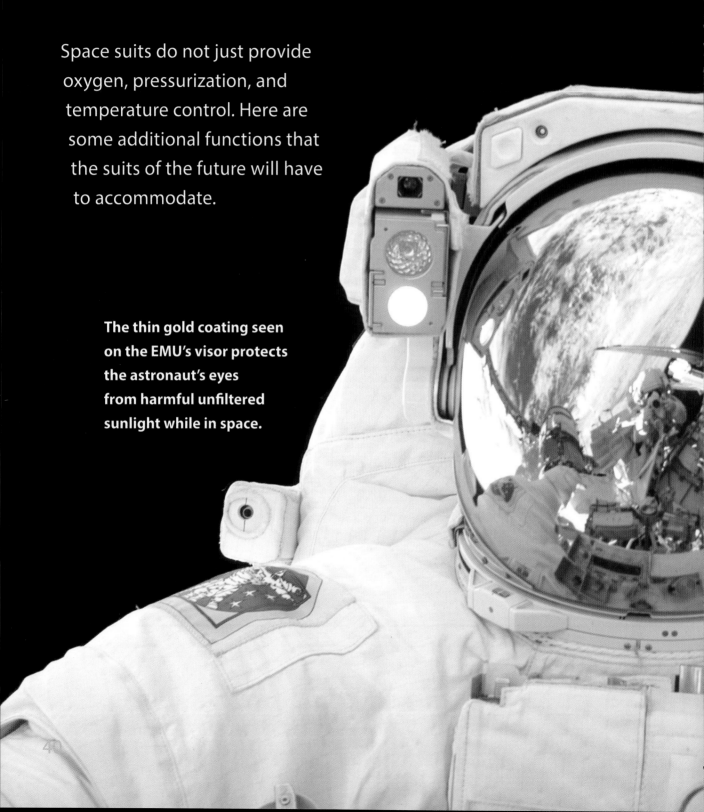

Space suits do not just provide oxygen, pressurization, and temperature control. Here are some additional functions that the suits of the future will have to accommodate.

The thin gold coating seen on the EMU's visor protects the astronaut's eyes from harmful unfiltered sunlight while in space.

Radiation protection. Earth's **atmosphere** helps protect us from invisible ultraviolet **radiation.** Without such protection, an astronaut in space might quickly suffer sunburn and tissue damage. Conventional space suits use thick layers of fabric, but offer little radiation protection. Many space suits include a special gold-plated visor that astronauts can pull down to shield their eyes from the glare of the sun. Newman and her team are working with industry partners to develop new radiation materials. By combining very lightweight materials called *aerogels* and *nanotubes*, they are working to create space suit components to protect astronauts from radiation during deep space missions.

Sensing. A space suit is packed with devices called **sensors** that monitor the performance of both the astronaut and the suit itself. Such sensors might, for example, detect a malfunction in the suit's heating and cooling system, alerting the astronaut to return to the protection of the spacecraft.

Comfort. Astronauts wear space suits for long periods, during which they may get hungry or thirsty or have to go to the bathroom. Most space suits have a nozzle in the helmet attached to a water supply. Thirsty astronauts can turn their head and suck on the nozzle for a drink. Some suits are designed to hold an energy bar that an astronaut could snack on in a similar way. But most astronauts just prefer to eat before their spacewalks. Astronauts wear a special absorbent undergarment—similar to a diaper—in case nature calls.

Collision protection.
Pieces of rock and debris whizz around space at thousands of miles or kilometers per hour. Earth's **atmosphere** shields us from most of these objects, which burn up long before they hit the ground. But, they pose a serious danger to astronauts in space. Space suits have a special layer meant to reduce the effects of an impact, but getting hit would still be an extremely serious situation.

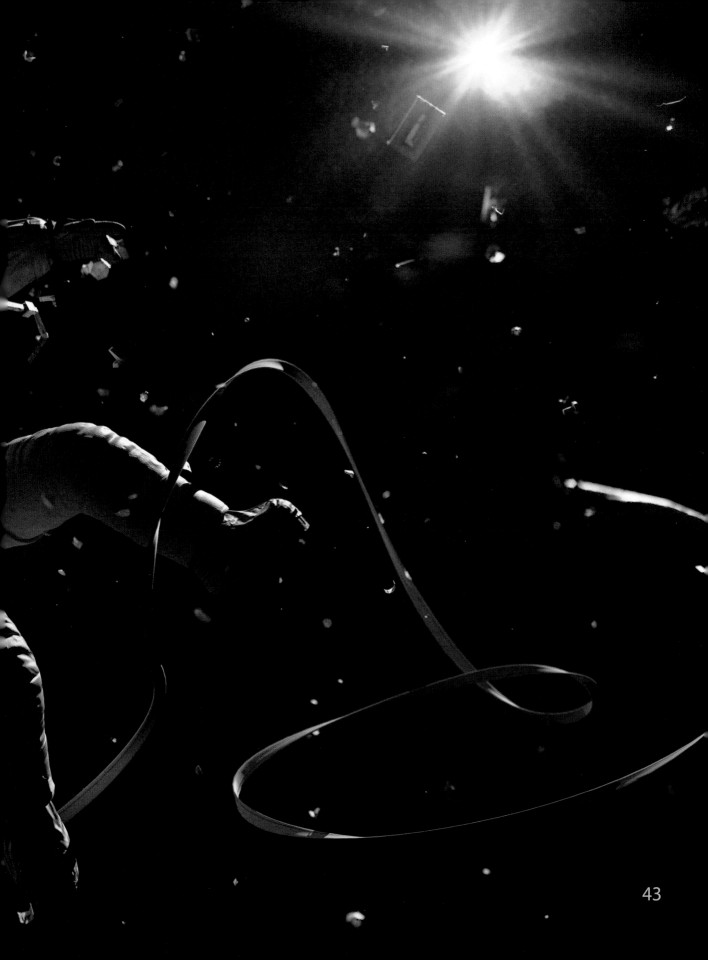

Dava Newman at work

**Dava Newman reviews BioSuit prototypes with former NASA
astronaut Mike Massimino.**

**Dava Newman and
Guillermo Trotti**

Glossary

aerospace the field of science, technology, and industry dealing with the flight of rockets and spacecraft through the atmosphere or the space beyond it.

atmosphere the mass of gases that surrounds a planet.

atom one of the most basic units of matter, consisting of a *nucleus* (core) of particles called *protons* and *neutrons* with tiny particles called *electrons* moving around the nucleus.

carbon dioxide a colorless, odorless gas present in the atmospheres of many planets, including Earth.

engineer a person who uses scientific principles to design structures, such as bridges and skyscrapers, machines, and all sorts of products.

gravitation also called **gravitational pull** or **force of gravity,** the force of attraction that acts between all objects because of their *mass,* or the amount of matter they contain. Because of gravitation, an object that is near Earth falls toward the surface of the planet. We experience this force on our bodies as our weight.

lines of nonextension bands of skin that may twist or turn but never stretch.

mechanical counterpressure (MCP) pressure provided by a material in direct contact with the skin, rather than by pressurized air.

molecule two or more atoms bonded together.

orbit a looping path around an object in space; the condition of circling a massive object in space under the influence of the object's gravity.

radiation energy given off in the form of waves or tiny particles of matter.

sensor a device that detects heat, light, or some other phenomenon, producing an electric signal.

shape memory materials a combination of metals or other materials that can "remember" its shape, returning to its original shape upon reaching a certain temperature.

vacuum empty space without even air in it.

Inventor challenge:
Space suits for Europa

Imagine that life has been discovered beneath the frozen crust of Jupiter's moon Europa. Astronauts are needed to operate the equipment to dig through the ice and study this life. How would you develop a new space suit for working on the surface of Europa, just like Dava Newman did for Mars?

STEP 1

Think about the challenge

Compile the environmental conditions of Europa, Earth, Mars, the moon, and the vacuum of space. Look up things like gravitational pull; atmospheric pressure; radiation; and temperature highs, lows, and averages. Gather information from reliable sources, such as World Book or NASA's website. Think about the kinds of work astronauts would have to do on Europa.

STEP 2

Create your prototype

Compare the conditions of Europa with the other places you looked up and the space suits designed for these places. Will you be able to use existing designs as a starting-off point, or will you have to come up with something different? Remember that Newman first studied hard suits for Mars. Would that idea work for Europa?

STEP 3

Share your design

Share your design with friends, classmates, or teachers. Give a presentation showing how it would work, like Newman has done with the BioSuit. See what your audience thinks could be improved. If possible, share your design with engineers and scientists and ask for their input.

STEP 4

Grow your idea

Ask the people who gave you advice to help you revise your prototype. Maybe you can create a wearable prototype with their help, like Newman did. Repeat until your space suit is ready for launch. Now you just have to wait for scientists to find life on Europa!

Index